Seizing the Crypto Bull Run for Financial Freedom

Get in Before the Crowd, out Before the Crash!

Deeann D. Mathews

ISBN: 978-1-7355752-1-6

Table of Contents

Introduction **4**

What I Am and What I Am Not, Upfront 4

What This Book Is and What It Is Not 5

Why Crypto, Anyway? 7

Chapter 1: Why Crypto Now? (In Your "Now") **12**

Chapter 2: But What Is Crypto, REALLY? **20**

The Story of Bitcoin, the First Electronic "Hard Money" 20

The Story of Ethereum and Its Extended Family 24

The Story of Hive, the Community Chain that Rescued Itself 27

Let's Review… 31

Chapter 3: Investment Principles and Decisions **33**

General Investment Principles to Remember 33

Decide Your Style: Are You More an Investor or a Trader? 34

What Makes for a Good Investment? 36

What Makes a Good Crypto Trader or Investor? 38

Chapter 4: Centralized and Decentralized Exchanges **40**

Centralized Exchanges (CEXes) 40

Decentralized Exchanges (or DEXes) 43

And Then There's the CEX in DEX's Clothing … 46

Chapter 5: Crypto Wallets, Hot and Cold **48**

But What Is a Crypto Wallet? 49

Chapter 6: Plan Your Exit FIRST **53**

Chapter 7: Now, Plan Your Entrance **59**

Chapter 8: My Personal Strategy **66**

Chapter 9: The SCBRFF Newsletter **72**

What the SCBRFF Newsletter Will Do for You 72

But WHY? 73

Your First Crypto-Related Call to Action! 74

One More Added-Value Thing… 75

Epilogue: Seizing the Best Possible Start on Hive **77**

You Are in the Matrix, For Real … 77

Ready To Own a Business and a Bank of Your Own? 78

Desktop/Laptop or Mobile? 81

Joining and Getting Your Keys 82

SCBRFF Tip 1: Free is Good, but Fast is BETTER 86

SCBRFF Tip No. 2: Be a Good Neighbor 90

SCBRFF Tip 3: The Big Four and Your Intro Post 92

SCBRFF Tip 4: The Square Deal Plan 97

The SCBRFF Exclusive Playlist on YouTube 101

Glossary of Terms 103

Introduction

Welcome to *Seizing the Crypto Bull Run for Financial Freedom*! If you have purchased this book, congratulations! You have separated yourself from the one-third of cryptocurrency investors who have no idea what they are doing. You have already decided not to be in those numbers! As you read, you will understand how far ahead you can go.

What I Am and What I Am Not, Upfront

I am not a financial advisor, nor am I a tax advisor. This guide is for informational purposes only, not professional advice. Although this guide provides helpful information on approaching the crypto markets best, this is not a substitute for financial advice. You should contact a financial or tax advisor if you choose to participate in the crypto markets, especially with the current uncertainty of crypto regulations.

Though I am not a financial advisor, I am a crypto investor who began my journey in 2019. If you are just now stepping into the crypto world, I have seen one more full cycle than you with results from this last cycle. The gains I have earned through my crypto journey have allowed me to sit here and work on this book (while others are working a 9-5). Despite making many mistakes and learning as I went, I achieved my first taste of financial freedom. Modest bill-paying money over a long time best describes how I made out in my first bull run.

For the record, no – I am not the world's leading expert in cryptocurrency. I'm also not driving a Lamborghini, nor have one to show you. That wasn't what I was after. I was more after the freedom to focus on the things I wanted to spend my time on. Also, I wanted it in a way that was not bound to everyday money or any particular country's declarations of who is worthy of freedom. After all, Bitcoin spends worldwide (and we'll get into how later).

I am, however, a woman who ventured into cryptocurrency looking for an avenue to greater personal and financial freedom, and guess what? I found it! I want you to know what I learned so you can be better prepared for the opportunities that financial freedom and location-independent income can give you. It will also help you generate a better investment and profit early in the coming bull cycle!

What This Book Is and What It Is Not

This book is a primer – a first educational resource – to help you understand how to get into the crypto bull run early and prepare to succeed. If you buy it before 2025, you will have ample time to build on this to get the most out of the bull run. If you purchase it later than Winter 2025, consider yourself getting set up for 2027 and 2028 (and I'll explain why in Chapter 1).

This book is a guide to show you the work you must do, but understand that handholding is not possible in crypto. Seizing the crypto bull run is something you will have to learn by *doing*. I will let you know where to find the tools you need. And if you read to the end, you'll find an extended resource to assist you. Because I made many mistakes between 2019 and 2021, I can steer you around many potholes on the road to the crypto bull run. It would be best if you still committed to getting up the road by:

- Exploring and learning about the tools;
- Choosing what tools are best for you and
- Consistently using them.

This book alone will not give you financial freedom; it is just a guide. Only you can do that by consistently and adequately using the tools here. You have the power, and this book and the newsletter are here to help you cultivate it. But you must seize the coming bull run for yourself!

Why Crypto, Anyway?

In short, cryptocurrency is a young, open market with assets within reach of Main Street. We can still get into this market with our everyday money and change our situation considerably! Imagine investing in Amazon or Apple before the first big tech boom. Yes, that would have been risky, and plenty of companies would have wasted your money. But, if you identified what made Amazon or Apple different, you would have been able to take a small amount of money and turn it into situation-changing money by now. Put a pin right here:

Pay attention to:

- The importance of understanding what to do early on;
- Investing reasonable amounts in promising projects and;
- Being patient in letting the market cycles do the work.

This book is coming out in Autumn 2023 to give you the earliest start on a bull run, likely starting in Spring 2024. If the charting patterns of the past hold up, the bull run will be between Spring 2024 and Autumn 2025.

In August 2023, when I am writing this, most cryptos are still well below 50 percent of their all-time highs from the top of the last bull run. Outside of Bitcoin, most are 70-90 percent below their highs.

The crypto market has been in a **bear market** (crashing and then sitting around its bottom) for about a year. People began to panic and exited the market. But the crowd will return once the stories of impressive gains emerge. By then, the better part of the fantastic gains will be in the hands of those who came in before the excited crowd.

I had the idea of this book because I walked into the crypto market in March 2019, during the last of the collapse. By the summer of that year, most people were running from crypto and talking about it being all over.

I'm here now because I never followed the crowd. I believed that I had found crypto at that time by no accident. I discovered that crypto has a four-year cycle, so I gritted my teeth, learned, made baby investments, and hung on. 2020 was right over the hill.

Crypto is in a bear market in 2023, and people are saying the same things they were saying in 2019. But 2024 and 2025 are right over the hill. Because I remember this feeling of doom and gloom but saw the light at the end of the tunnel, I want you to see that light, too.

There is one significant difference between 2019 and 2023, however. Since the last bull run, governments and corporations have certainly noticed the potential for everyday people to change their financial and therefore living situations through crypto, potential that has nothing to do with plugging into a corporate job, the regular movement of money through the banking system, or even the political cycles that overlap the crypto cycles.

Governments and corporations are not necessary a friend to the freedom crypto can bring to the people, and they are beginning to show what they would like to do to restrict that freedom. There is a ton of conversation about regulation now, which has some good and bad sides. Still, the net result may be that some assets will be unavailable for regular people to invest in for "safety reasons." Other assets that miss that designation will become too expensive to access without mediation from large financial institutions.

Don't get me wrong: I'm not saying that regulation and the traditional financial institutions that broker things like stocks, bonds, and real estate are all bad. But because the people who make regulations have their campaigns paid for by those in traditional financial institutions and corporations, Wall Street gets favored over Main Street in every market whose shape is dominated by said regulations and institutions.

Regulations are also shaped by the disaster that often happens to "crowd investors." These people tend to come in late in an asset or market's run with more hopes and dreams than knowledge, invest amounts they cannot afford to lose, and then lose it all in the crash. This phenomenon allows governments to enact hard-core regulations and turn markets over to the approved institutional players. (Note: none of those parties want us to be too independent from them.) Thus, the crowd's behavior gives governments publicly acceptable reasons to remove opportunities from our reach.

"Crowd investors" do need protection. However, individual investors need to *get in before the crowd and get out before the crash.* Here's why: this cycle's markets may be extra wild because this may be the last run before heavy regulation and institutional control take significant gains out of individual investors' reach.

Knowledge is power – power to seize opportunities and build protection in advance from difficult situations. Most people will not consider investing in Bitcoin or other cryptocurrencies until Bitcoin makes the news at some high price milestone late next year or early in 2025. But by the time that price milestone occurs, much of the opportunity in the market will be gone.

This is why I am glad you have picked up this book now (which I will call *your "now"*), whenever that might happen to be. Even if you do not get this book until 2025, you will still be ahead of the crowd of 2028. By the end of this book, you will learn:

- What crypto is;
- The cycles it historically follows;
- How to find and understand good projects and;
- How to get in and out ahead of the crash and enjoy financial freedom while others flounder.

Let's get started (and, note that you can find all bold-faced terms in this book that are new to you in the Glossary at the end for more explanation)!

Chapter 1: Why Crypto Now? (In Your "Now")

If you watch the regular news, online or offline, the last time you heard about crypto was a disaster. Sam Bankman-Fried – founder of the crypto exchange FTX – allegedly mismanaged investor funds. This created a chain reaction of events leading to its demise and the loss of investors' money. He is currently awaiting trial. That was the last big story at the time of this writing.

If you follow politics and finance, you may have heard about several banks struggling with liquidity issues. You may have heard talks about crypto needing regulation because of Sam and a few other bad actors.

It may have been a while since you've heard the name Bitcoin in widespread discussion. The reason for all this is *timing*.

The crypto market follows Bitcoin, and every four years, Bitcoin goes through what is called its **halving event.** Only half as much Bitcoin is available for mining after each halving event. There will only ever be 21 million Bitcoins. So, not only is the supply running out, but the amount available every four years is shrinking by half.

This leads to something called a **supply shock** in the crypto markets. It tends to be the catalyst for investors to enter the market. Remembering that fresh Bitcoin will not always be available, investors start the scramble into the market. Then, some of their investment money will move to younger and less expensive projects. This is where the bull run kicks off.

In previous cycles, it has been typical for the crypto markets to grow for a year and a half after the halving event, and the halving event is where most people who understand the crypto cycle enter. The average investors, on the other hand, tends to get in a year later. They hear stories of the fantastic gains from the year of the halving. They feel like that is the right time to enter the market. For a while, no matter what people invest in, it seems that nothing can go wrong. Money is everywhere in abundance; everyone is a genius at investing. The news grows and pulls more people in. More and more people look to double, triple, 10x, 100x, or 1000x their investment like they heard others were doing.

Unfortunately, most gains are over by the time the average investor picks up the market news. The early investors, big and small, sell to later-coming ones and count their money. Experienced crypto investors know what will happen next: about a year and a half after the halving event, Bitcoin will top out. Within two years, all the coins that followed Bitcoin up will top out, and then the crash will begin the bear market.

Because I came into the crypto markets in 2019, I have experienced two bear sides of the cycle. Can you say, "Two years of pain and suffering"? I missed 2018 but did not miss 2022 and 2023, which were painful. Bitcoin lost 70 percent of its value. Some **altcoins** – all crypto coins that are not Bitcoin – lost up to 95-99 percent of their value.

Imagine that you came into the market in the winter of 2022, having no idea what was coming in the spring. You're buying on hopes and dreams, hoping that the latest dip means an opportunity to get better gains in the future. But then, you see every dollar you invested drop to ten cents or less in the coming year. The following year, it stays down. Many people went through that in 2022. They did not know there is a light at the end of the tunnel as 2023 starts to move to a close and 2024 approaches.

Hence why I call this chapter "Why Crypto Now?" I am writing this for you in Summer 2023, so the earliest possible "Now" is Autumn 2023. This is the perfect time for you to situate yourself in the markets.

I remember thinking in the summer of 2020, "If only I had known in the summer of 2019 what I know now … but I will be ready in 2023, next time around." You will get to say that in 2027 because you, too, will be an experienced investor! But in the meantime, let's discuss *your "now"* and what to expect:

- **Autumn 2023 to early Spring 2024, before the halving:**

If this is *your "now"* and you are new, this is the perfect time to learn about crypto and make basic investments. Some basics that you will need to learn are:

  - how the markets work,
  - how wallets and custody work, and
  - what your personal trading and investing style is.

The end of the bear market is the best time for more experienced investors to invest for the biggest gains. But if you are new, focus on learning. You still have time to make large gains because you are ahead of the new cycle.

- **Late Spring 2024 to Autumn 2024, up to six months after the halving:**

If this is *your "now,"* you are still early and need to learn about crypto and understand how everything I mentioned above works. However, putting more time and intensity into your learning would be best. I came into the markets at this same point in the summer of 2020 and did not invest until the early autumn. I still get to sit and write this for you at whatever hour I want, so don't panic. You are early in the new cycle and still ahead of most everyday investors. Significant gains in slower-moving projects will still be possible.

- **Late Autumn 2024 to end of Spring 2025:**

If this is *your "now,"* you are most likely in the heart of the bull run proper. You are beginning to hear about the early significant gains that people who got in ahead of you are having. You still have to learn everything everyone who came before you needed to, but at least much more information will be available. The main thing for you to remember is this: *don't get greedy*. The crypto you are about to buy will be sold to you by someone who got those 10x to 100x gains everyone around you is talking about. But that time in the cycle, particularly if you are at the Spring end of this period, is past. However, if you are at the autumn or winter portions of this time, there will most likely be good projects that can double or triple your investment. Focus on learning how to find good projects. You can still see large gains by being diligent. Just *don't get greedy.*

- **Summer 2025:**

If this is *your "now,"* everyone seems to be talking about crypto, and the stories of significant gains are all around you. Yet, as I said before, every bit of crypto you buy will be sold to you by the people who have those gains and are getting out. Take the advice *"don't get greedy"* even more seriously. Many projects will likely have one more jump up to the top of the bull run in the autumn. If you go back and look at those projects that got off to a late start compared to when others started running, you may still be able to secure large gains. However, you need to realize that the bull run is most likely almost over. *Whatever you do, do not get greedy here.*

If you pick this book up in Autumn 2025 or later, know that by mid-autumn, you will be hearing more about crypto than you ever have. Big-time investors will be flooding the news so that people like you can buy crypto at the top of the market so they can get out at the top. They are leaving you to endure the coming crash. If you are in September or October of 2025, the exact top may have yet to come. The fact that the top has occurred and passed may not be obvious even into Spring 2026. But if you look at the charts or track the price in Winter 2026, you may see a persistent downtrend has formed. That means there are more sellers than buyers. Eventually, the panic will set in when people finally realize the bears have arrived. Those bears will eat well through 2026 and not be full (when the market finds the bottom) until at least mid-2027.

Needless to say, the autumn of 2025 to the summer of 2027 might not be the best time to start investing in crypto. But you can read this book and get ready for the next cycle!

This book will be promoted primarily from the autumn of 2023 to the autumn of 2024 because I want readers to get the most out of it. If the cycle patterns hold, and you can be ready to make moves around the turn of 2025, you will undoubtedly do well. There will be enough of a run left to reward your learning and your choice of investment. As said about many other types of investments, *time in the market is more important than timing the market.* For crypto, in particular: “buying the dip” is less important than knowing *where* that dip in price comes from in the four-year cycle.

I am publishing this book in the autumn of 2023 because it is the ideal time for new investors to learn. Just as experienced investors begin investing toward the new cycle, the earlier you understand what to do and do it, the more run you have ahead of you for investment and profit. Also, this means you will need to invest less money to see substantial gains. You also may get some tax advantages for being an early bird, and I'll cover that in a later chapter. Whenever *your "now"* may happen to be, you have given yourself an advantage over the crowd by choosing to educate yourself through reading this book – so let's keep going!

Chapter 2: But What Is Crypto, REALLY?

One of the most important but neglected principles of sound investing is "Never invest in anything you don't understand." This principle is often ignored in the crypto space. By the time Bitcoin hits the news again, your local corner store may have a kiosk for you to buy Bitcoin. Mine does. I remember when that feature arrived in the last cycle, too – just in time to get in and lose money. People who genuinely love Bitcoin will tell you that it's not about the value in fiat currency. It's about the fact that Bitcoin is the world's first "**hard money**." This is opposed to the "**soft money**" printed by governments not using a gold or silver standard to back their currencies up, and with no limit to how many units of it that can be printed. The story of Bitcoin and two other examples will give you an understanding of the crypto world and why it functions the way it does.

The Story of Bitcoin, the First Electronic "Hard Money"

The story goes (and you'll find it in the "White Paper" section on https://bitcoin.org/en/) that around 2008, a gentleman or a group of individuals calling themselves "Satoshi Nakamoto" observed something during the Great Recession. The banks and the mortgage companies had wrecked the global economy by giving mortgages out to people who couldn't or wouldn't pay for them. Then, those mortgages were traded at dozens and even hundreds of times their actual value. These banks fell, but most avoided total collapse due to government bailouts. They did not collapse because of their foolishness but because the governments judged them "too big to fail." Unfortunately, everyday people had to pick up the pieces of the wrecked economy.

But how was this bailout possible? Satoshi Nakamoto realized that governments could always find money because they could print it on demand. Without the inconvenience of needing to have each unit of a currency backed by gold or silver or any hard asset, the governments could pay off bills of any size. The problem with this massive print run – called money supply inflation – is that unbacked currencies lose their value as the supply increases. Inflation robs fiat currencies of their purchasing power. People need more and more units of that currency to exchange for the hard value of goods and services. In other words, everything real costs more because of the inflation of fiat currencies. Over time, those currencies can become worthless.

The net result of the Great Recession was that everyday people paid twice. Firstly, for the banks' damage to the whole economy. Secondly, inflated currencies had less purchasing power because governments chose to print their way out instead of letting the banks fail. Satoshi Nakamoto also realized that nothing in the entire global monetary system could stop governments and banks from doing this dance repeatedly until every currency with an unlimited, unbacked supply was worthless, leaving everyday people impoverished.

Satoshi Nakamoto decided that enough was enough. He took his (or their) computer science skills – cryptography in particular – to design a kind of electronic, hard money defined by code that had to be deciphered. Since computers operate in bits and bytes, the name "**Bitcoin**" emerged. The code was set up to allow anyone with computing power to tap into the open-source system and crack a **cryptographic hash** (a piece of protected code) to claim a portion of Bitcoin. This was called "**electronic mining**."

System users could validate the work done and allow the claim to be recorded on the system. The recordings are called a **ledger**, but not like the ones used in business. Everyone working to mine Bitcoin could see the work done and its accuracy in the open ledger, so there was no chance of anyone cheating. Because the open ledger was present with the system on every validator's computer, the only way to shut down the design and record would be to shut down every computer running it. This also gave Bitcoin the advantage of being community-owned, community-run, and **decentralized** – meaning no single entity can be shut down to shut it down.

Because the pieces of hash presented themselves in big blocks of text, and because one block after another appeared like chain links, this new technology that emerged was dubbed "the **blockchain**." Bitcoin – the first cryptocurrency – is also the first blockchain system.

The problem Bitcoin is designed to solve is to be "hard money," which removes the inflationary printing of currency. It will never inflate because only 21 million completed transactions to make a Bitcoin will ever be mined. There will only ever be 21 million total Bitcoins, divided into eight places called "**Satoshis**" – in honor of its inventor(s). By comparison, the U.S. dollar is divided into one hundred cents. Each Bitcoin is divided into 100 million Satoshis, so there is enough of it to go around so everyone can get a little. But when it is all mined and bought up, that's it. Scarcity is the "hard backing" of its value.

One of the criticisms of Bitcoin is that, after all, it's just electronic "hash." It's not gold or silver or what we think of as currency in everyday use. But then again, your plastic credit and debit cards connect to electronic systems that transfer whatever your bank or credit card company says you have in fiat dollars. Because we all believe this electronic process and the currencies the process connects to are real, we can slide pieces of plastic into things and receive goods and services. Or we can type in a series of numbers from those pieces of plastic into our computers or phones and receive goods and services.

The difference is that our plastic and numbers are connected to a system backed by a currency constantly inflating and losing value. Bitcoin's "hash" represents a non-inflationary value that, although it goes up and down with the markets, is likely to increase dramatically over time. This is because enough people have chosen to believe in a future where this type of money holds its value. Its movements are transparent. Anyone without reference to a centralized government or financial system can get access.

Understand as we prepare to move on that Bitcoin is called a "**Proof-of-Work**" blockchain: value is created by the work done by decoding hashes that are validated to release Bitcoin to the miner. Most early blockchains, including **Ethereum** – the second fundamental cryptocurrency – followed this pattern.

The Story of Ethereum and Its Extended Family

The first thing to understand here is this: in crypto, everything that is not Bitcoin is called an "**altcoin**." Altcoin is short for alternative coin, and the most important of these is Ethereum.

Sometime after Bitcoin was up and running (you'll find more about this in the "Learn" section on https://ethereum.org/en/), a team led by Vitalik Buterin looked at Bitcoin and said, "This is great that we have decentralized hard money. But we need decentralized businesses and applications to spend it in, and we can't build these on Bitcoin." So in 2015, they launched Ethereum, whose code contained the ability for other developers to build decentralized applications – called "**dapps**" as opposed to apps – on the blockchain.

Ethereum is the first blockchain that is referred to as a **Layer 1**. It is the base for all the other applications built on it and many other projects and cryptocurrencies that run on the Ethereum blockchain. Those projects are often referred to as **Layer 2** projects. My Google search at the time of this writing shows that thousands of projects are running on Ethereum that use **ETH** (the currency) itself to do transactions. Then, some projects have their own cryptocurrencies that also run on Ethereum – cryptocurrencies backed by Ethereum! Then, some cryptocurrencies started on Ethereum and became their own independent blockchains. So, one has the Ethereum ecosystem proper and the ecosystems that are its "offspring." Together, the Ethereum Extended Family, as I like to think of all these projects and cryptocurrencies, dominate many of the top 100 rankings of cryptocurrencies in the world.

One of the challenges of Ethereum is that so many people run transactions that the chain can get slow. People are willing to pay high transaction fees to validators to make things happen more quickly. These fees are called **gas fees**, and they can get ridiculously high.

You must account for the gas fees to do anything when you buy Ethereum and coins that run on Ethereum. I used to wait until the middle of the night to buy Ethereum ecosystem coins on Ethereum-based decentralized exchanges and move them into my wallets. Many cryptocurrencies in the Ethereum ecosystem were created to find ways around the congestion and fees, and many projects considered to be Ethereum alternatives (like Cardano, Polkadot, and the Binance Smart Chain) initially came to be for the same reason. However, Ethereum still holds the number two spot after Bitcoin for importance because of its proven security, utility, and durability.

Ethereum is also one of the few chains that began as Proof-of-Work and went to **Proof-of-Stake**. Mining of Ethereum hashes has ceased.

Instead, validators have to have a certain amount of ETH saved on the chain – called **staking** – to participate in keeping the blocks going and earning fresh Ethereum. This change took place in 2022, bringing Ethereum in line with many younger projects that began as Proof-of-Stake projects. These types of projects define who validates transactions on the chain based on how much of the cryptocurrency is saved or staked on the chain.

Bitcoin has been blessed with some creative developers, and now, like Ethereum, does have some dapps related to its purpose as hard, transparent money running on it. Unfortunately, it also has transaction fees that reflect its increasing usage since it began. Both can get relatively slow and have high transaction fees. Unless you have money in hand, you will find it very hard to access them. Bitcoin mining is now a big, complicated business, and Ethereum mining is no more. Solving the problem of access to cryptocurrency for those without purchasing power for the coins, the fees, or expensive equipment is now beyond Bitcoin and Ethereum. However, there are cryptocurrencies designed to meet these needs, and the best of these is Hive.

The Story of Hive, the Community Chain that Rescued Itself

To understand the story of Hive, first know that a blockchain can do something called "**forking.**" Suppose enough members of a particular project's community want to go in a different direction than the initial project. In that case, they can start a new project by branching off the old one – same technology, new direction. Bitcoin has two well-known forks available as cryptocurrencies that can be bought today: Bitcoin Cash and Bitcoin SV. Ethereum has one well-known fork called Ethereum Classic. Over time, as different developers work on the forked chains, they develop unique elements and are the sources of much discussion about which fork better upholds the original vision. Bitcoin S(atoshi) V(ision) and Ethereum Classic, by their choice of names, seem to be asserting that they represent the true vision of their originating project better than what their originating projects have now become.

But then you have those cases in which the community that built a fork shouts back at the originating project: "We're nothing like you! We're keeping all the values of decentralization, community, honesty, and fair play you gave up!" That was more or less how Hive forked from its predecessor, Steem, in 2020.

Both Steem and Hive are what is called "**Proof-of-Brain**" blockchains. If you have time, a device that can access regular social media, and the ability to create good content, Steem and Hive's social media front-ends allow users to get an account and post into different communities. Users earn Steem or Hive based on the community upvoting their work. Both chains retain some Proof-of-Stake features: the more Steem or Hive you have staked on the chain, the more Steem or Hive you can mine for someone else by voting for their content. The idea of Proof-of-Brain stands out because even people who do not have money can turn their creativity into access to cryptocurrency from anywhere in the world with an internet connection. They can also retain ownership of their intellectual property.

Since 2020, Hive has distinguished itself from Steem by its diverse and robust ecosystem of video, audio, and mixed-media front ends. This front-end hosts:

- different interests and niches
- games
- NFTs (think art on the blockchain if you have never heard of Non-Fungible Tokens)
- Marketplaces, and other dapps, many of which have Layer 2 tokens that can be both traded and received as rewards on posts

Transaction fees do not exist on Hive. There has also yet to be any of the slowing so common on Bitcoin and Ethereum. New developers have addressed this problem well.

But the main point about Hive, especially in Autumn 2023, is this: Even if you have no investment money at all but have a knack for long or short-form written content, audio or video creation, visual art, or mixed-media presentations, you can get your crypto sweat equity—Hive exchanges for both Bitcoin and Ethereum in quite a few markets around the world.

Hive is what you do when you have more time and creativity than money and you want to learn and grow in crypto with those doing the same. Although granted, because Hive's community is not tolerant of a lot of the foolishness that goes on elsewhere on the Internet, a walkthrough will help you get started right. This book's epilogue will guide you to get started on Hive if you want to learn crypto by earning and doing in the community.

Now, all disclosures: I am an investor in Hive. I began writing on Steem in 2019 to build up crypto sweat equity (since I did not understand crypto well enough yet to put money in, but I'm a reasonably good writer), and then moved over to Hive in 2020 when it was founded. My Steem paid for my first Bitcoin, which also paid for my first Ethereum. So, for me, Proof-of-Brain was my entry point into crypto.

I moved over to Hive because the community that forked it rescued this excellent democratizing model for crypto from new ownership on Steem that seemed to care nothing for democracy. I believe in financial freedom and global accessibility to means to earn without giving up one's intellectual property or soul. In that sense, Hive follows much of the original vision for cryptocurrency.

Let's Review…

- Bitcoin is the first cryptocurrency and blockchain and was designed to provide hard, transparent, decentralized money not subject to inflation, centralized oversight, and financial sleight-of-hand.
- Everything not Bitcoin is called an "altcoin," or alternative coin
- Ethereum was designed to allow other developers to build decentralized applications or dapps and is the Layer 1 or base layer to an ecosystem of other projects and coins.
- Layer 2 projects are applications built on a Layer 1 blockchain. Layer 2 coins run on the parent blockchain and are backed by the parent token. Ethereum is the model for this kind of cryptocurrency.

- Bitcoin is still a Proof-of-Work blockchain, meaning it must be electronically mined. But Ethereum is now Proof-of-Stake, meaning those who keep the chain going have a certain amount of ETH saved (staked) on the chain and earn ETH by validating the transactions going through.
- Hive is a Proof-of-Brain blockchain, meaning that people "mine" Hive based on the quality of their creative content in conjunction with the community on Hive's social media front-ends.
- Members of the Hive community give votes on user content with the value of that vote based on how much Hive they have staked, and this allows users to gain entry into crypto without needing to invest fiat currency upfront.
- Like Ethereum, Hive also has gaming, NFT art applications, decentralized exchanges, and other e-marketplaces.
- Unlike Ethereum, Hive has no transaction fees and speed that is not likely to decrease as Hive grows in usage.
- Most cryptos follow either the Proof-of-Work, Proof-of-Stake, or Proof-of-Brain model.

Chapter 3: Investment Principles and Decisions

"If you have six hours to cut down a tree,

spend four hours sharpening the axe."

– Abraham Lincoln, 16th president of the United States

I am writing this in Summer 2023 for launch in Autumn 2023. If you are reading this upon release, consider yourself in the axe-sharpening stage in the crypto cycle. If you pick this up later, however, no worries. No matter when you pick this up, the more prepared you are to make powerful moves before entering the market, the better off you will be.

General Investment Principles to Remember

- NEVER EVER invest in anything you don't understand.

- NEVER EVER invest more money in anything than you can afford to lose. (This is why starting early in the cycle is key.)

- Time in the market is more important than timing the market. (Riding the cycle wave means the market will do the work to get you investment and profit).

- Buy low, sell high – get in and out at the appropriate time to profit. (Another reason starting early in the cycle while prices are low is key.)

Decide Your Style: Are You More an Investor or a Trader?

- Traders in the crypto market focus on understanding a coin's price and what the project is doing to catch moves in the market to profit:

    - **Short-term traders** focus on days and weeks. They tend to focus on charts and technical investing, looking for indicators and patterns to see what the market will do next.

        - Advantage: getting profit and getting out more quickly.

        - Disadvantage: missing out on tax benefits to a more prolonged hold of a project.

    - **Long-term traders** focus on the length of the cycle. They want to get in early, put their money in, and let the market do the work. They tend to look more at fundamental investing, the project's chances to do what it promises, and where it is positioned relative to similar projects in the markets.

        - Advantage: tax benefits and maximizing long-term profits.

        - Disadvantage: your money is tied down for long periods of time, and you potentially lose out on newer opportunities.

- Both sets of traders are more concerned about price moves than the long-term mission of the project; the time scales are just different.

- True investors in the crypto market are looking for projects they want to see succeed in the world. Also, they want to use their resources to build up the projects they believe in with less concern for immediate profit.

- Yet, even investors consider profit-taking through interest and growth at the appropriate times in the market.

- If you decide to be more of a trader, focus on understanding how crypto moves in the time scale you are interested in and have your exit plan done before entering the markets.

- If you decide to be more of an investor, prepare standards for profit-taking and a final exit. That exit may be far down the road, but the way crypto is, it is better to be ready sooner than later.

What Makes for a Good Investment?

Bitcoin and Ethereum are good places to start because they have proven their utility and resilience. Hive can also be an excellent place to start if you need crypto sweat equity.

- A good crypto investment has utility: the project addresses a need in the world or crypto world and provides a solution. Bitcoin addresses the need for better money, and Ethereum the need for space to build e-commerce in a decentralized way.

- A good crypto investment has usage if it is an established project. Even in the bear market, it should have (or should have had, if you see this in the summer of 2024 or later) developers and a community user base upholding, improving, and expanding the utility of the project.

- A good crypto investment will have a good leadership team, especially if the project is new. That team needs to have a track record of success in areas related to what the crypto project is meant to do.

- A great crypto investment aligns with existing regulations, although in some countries, this is more challenging than in others. In the U.S., only Bitcoin and Ethereum have successfully passed the designation "unregistered securities". This means the SEC will not be attempting to shut them down. (Another reason to start with Bitcoin and Ethereum while the SEC and the crypto industry work out the status of the other altcoins.)

What Makes a Good Crypto Trader or Investor?

- Both understand that they do not need to invest more than they can afford.

- Both make it their business to understand the length of time in the cycle they want to be in and how crypto projects tend to behave on those time scales.

- Both make it their business to assess where news and regulations are and control their risks based on getting that knowledge.

- Both understand that if a crypto project does not have utility, usage, and a strong leadership team, no matter the hype around a coin from a loud community, that project might not be the best choice in the long term. It can, however, be okay for short-term trades.

- Both understand the importance of not being greedy and of making plans to enter and exit the market at the appropriate time in the cycle.

Chapter 4: Centralized and Decentralized Exchanges

The main places where people get their crypto are from **crypto exchanges**. Crypto exchanges are places where one can buy crypto with **fiat money** (everyday money) and exchange cryptos for one another. Generally, exchanges are set up such that you can buy cryptos for everyday money, with **stablecoins** (crypto coins backed and pegged to the local currency, one for one). They can often be purchased with Bitcoin and Ethereum. (Another reason to begin investing with them: the increases in the price of Bitcoin and Ethereum can bring you profit and give you investment resources for other projects.)

Centralized Exchanges (CEXes)

Most people begin their journey buying cryptos on **centralized exchanges**. These are called "centralized" because they have a central point of control. They are generally owned by a corporation and operate under the laws of the country they are opened in. The United States is particularly picky, so I have included five big ones available around the world that are available here:

- Kraken
- Binance.us
- Coinbase
- eToro
- Gate.us

Notice that ".us" bit on the end? The United States would have liked to have shut almost all crypto exchanges down. Even with its Securities and Exchange Commission receiving enormous pushback from the crypto industry and community, it has been able to impose considerable restrictions on centralized exchanges and, therefore, on access to crypto by U.S. citizens! Some exchanges have needed to create those .us front-ends even to operate in compliance in the U.S.

This is another reason to focus on Bitcoin and Ethereum in these early stages. They are among the coins the SEC has not decided to classify as "unregistered securities." If you pick this book up in mid-2024 or later, the regulatory situation may have cleared up, and all may be well for a number of coins. But at the time of this writing, in Summer 2023, the SEC and the crypto industry are still working things out. So, the safest two coins to start learning and investing in are Bitcoin and Ethereum.

And then there is the whole "Know Your Customer/Anti-Money Laundering" (KYC/AML) issue on centralized exchanges. If you get around freedom and privacy-minded crypto investors and whisper "KYC/AML," you will send their blood pressure up for a good reason!

Centralized exchanges that allow U.S. citizens to use them make users suffer from the legacy of bad actors who have used crypto for evil. So now, everyone in the U.S. using these exchanges must shell out a lot of personal information to prove their identity. You'll have to turn over a copy of your driver's license or passport, and sometimes bank statements and proof of address in addition to your tax ID to access the markets through these exchanges. These exchanges report your moves to the IRS about how much you make, just like your job records. They also hold onto your personal information. Not only does this leave room for your crypto and buying data to be hacked from exchanges, but your identifying documents and banking information are also at risk. You must trust the exchange to secure your identity and crypto because you can go broke both ways if they don't!

To their credit, crypto exchanges, like banks, take considerable security measures. A centralized exchange has rarely failed or gone through a total hack. The crypto market, however, is still small and has yet to be a significant target for cybercrime. That will change as institutional money moves into Bitcoin, Ethereum, and possibly the Ethereum Extended Family. So, although centralized exchanges are the easiest and most readily available place to start buying crypto, certain risks are attached. This is why it is essential to know about…

Decentralized Exchanges (or DEXes)

No one owns **decentralized exchanges**; they run on programs on particular blockchains. Ethereum is the king of hosting decentralized exchanges, but members of the Ethereum Extended Family also host some of these, as does Hive.

Decentralized exchanges have no means or need to check for who or where you are. You attach the crypto wallet of your choice (we'll cover that in the next chapter), exchange the Layer 1 coin for the coin you want, and go from there. Some exchanges that work between wallets also allow you to buy Bitcoin or Ethereum with a credit or debit card, so you can use your purchased coins to exchange for other things.

The main advantage of decentralized exchanges is that you don't need to turn over your info and have it sitting on a server somewhere. (But please understand that Uncle Sam in the U.S. and his counterparts elsewhere in the world can still find you in terms of tracking your purchases and assessing your taxes if they really want to.)

The main disadvantage of a decentralized exchange is the same as the advantage: there is no one to collect your information. Generally, customer service is staffed just as well. Blockchain transactions are just about immutable. (Not quite, but rarely are they rolled back or forked because an individual didn't follow procedure and lost their crypto.) If you mess up on a decentralized exchange, that's too bad. Freedom isn't free. The price you pay for not having people in your crypto business on an exchange is that your losses are also nobody's business (except, maybe, Uncle Sam's, if he is even interested enough to bother).

Some of the better-known decentralized exchanges include:

- Uniswap (runs on Ethereum)

- 1Inch (runs on Ethereum)

- Wyre (runs inside the Metamask wallet so that you can buy Ethereum with everyday money)

- Simplex (large spread of cryptos available)

- Simpleswap (large spread of cryptos available, including Hive)

- Bisq (technically a web-based wallet, but you can buy and trade Bitcoin in it)

- Ionomy (large spread of cryptos available, including Hive)

- Hive Engine (runs on Hive for Hive projects)

- Tribaldex (runs on Hive for Hive projects)

And Then There's the CEX in DEX's Clothing …

There is another system that resembles Ethereum-type decentralized exchanges but is owned by Binance: the Binance Smart Chain (BSC). The BSC also connects to the Metamask wallet. The problem is that the BSC is owned and controlled by Binance, so although it looks like a DEX, it is an extension of a centralized exchange in disguise! I do not use the BSC … but it might look appealing when you get tired enough of Ethereum fees on most DEXes.

I promise I won't judge if you find some projects you like on Pancakeswap, which runs on the BSC. Just be aware that the BSC does not require KYC/AML and gives you access to certain Binance exchange offerings that may or may not be available on Binance.us. Freedom isn't free. You will quickly discover that the BSC merry-go-round will have you thinking you are buying the same coins you can get from an Ethereum Extended Family type of exchange, only to find out those coins cannot leave the BSC because they are encoded on it. You will then have to figure out how to exchange them for BNB, get up on Binance.us, and HOPE you can get your BNB swapped back there and sold. What Ethereum costs you in fees, it saves you in steps to perform and points where things can go horribly wrong on the BSC.

Ethereum's high cost also prevents the straight scamming that happened on the BSC in the last bull run. I remember the point at which scam coins were being minted and put out on the BSC every five minutes. In those days, I was a moderator on Reddit in a crypto subreddit. I used to go on Pancakeswap and check the numbers on BSC projects. Let's just say that there were more ways to get scammed on the BSC than the whole subreddit could keep up with.

Binance owns the BSC, but there is one way in which the BSC's disguise as a DEX is perfect: there are exactly as many customer service representatives on the BSC as people are taking your information for KYC/AML. There are just about as many people keeping scammers off the chain. I prefer to think of that reality in terms of the old baseball anthem: "And it's ONE, TWO, THREE strikes the BSC is out at the old ballgame!" That doesn't sing quite right, but let the off-putting nature of that stick in your mind about why I neither use nor recommend the BSC or any of its projects.

Chapter 5: Crypto Wallets, Hot and Cold

The first principle of being in the crypto space is this: *Don't leave your crypto on an exchange!* Buy it there, but take it off that exchange into your custody choice -- your own wallet.

Why, you may ask? Leaving your crypto on an exchange where you can sell it at a profit at the touch of a button might make sense if you are new. But remember: even if you read this in Autumn 2024 (the last time it will be promoted widely), you are still relatively early, and the top of the market may still be a year away. If your style is short-term trading, that may not matter to you. But if you have a longer-term view, leaving your crypto on an exchange is not the best idea.

Exchanges do fail. FTX is a big failure – $200 billion worth of failure – for the cycle we are leaving behind. It will be years before all that is worked out in the courts, and there is no guarantee anyone who had their crypto there will recover.

Exchanges do cut and run from lousy regulation situations. The SEC tried to shut down Kraken and Coinbase in the United States. Kraken settled, and Coinbase is still in court but operating at the time of this writing. But exchanges like Bittrex closed their doors to U.S. citizens, while others closed down entirely. This left people without crypto wallets and nowhere to go.

But What Is a Crypto Wallet?

The easiest way to understand a **crypto wallet** is this: a web-based or hardware-based application that interacts with various blockchains like an online bank account. These blockchains have addresses for users that record how much of a particular crypto that user has. The addresses are long strings of code that correspond with information on a specific blockchain. Every exchange has addresses like that, too. So, people send their crypto from one address to another on the blockchains their cryptos run on. A crypto wallet keeps track of the addresses on each blockchain that record how much crypto you own.

When you buy your crypto on an exchange, you can send it from the exchange address to your wallet address. When you are ready to sell your crypto, you can return it to the exchange address from your wallet address. In the meantime, your crypto is in your custody, in your wallet, away from the hustle and bustle of the market and its bad actors.

Regarding security, "**hot**" web-based wallets are easier to use. However, they are less secure than "**cold**" hardware wallets. Cold wallets can plug and unplug from the computer like a flash drive and be put away somewhere safe. They have backup phrases that you are asked to write down (in case your computer or hardware crashes) to recover your wallet and its info on the blockchain on your new system. Make sure you write that phrase down or type it and print it, then put it in a secure place. Do not leave these phrases saved in a file on a computer constantly in contact with the Internet. The hack attacks are coming for crypto wallets in the next bull run.

Some readily available wallets include:

- Metamask (decentralized, web-based. Runs as a plugin on many browsers. Comes set up for Ethereum but can also be set up for Polygon and BSC, and also has Wyre exchange built-in)

- Atomic (web-based. Downloads front-end to your computer. Has Simplex built-in)

- Bisq (decentralized, web-based. Set up for Bitcoin. Allows swapping for many other coins)

- Wirex (web-based. Downloads front-end to your phone or computer. Connects with Visa, Mastercard, and several DeFi and staking options)

- Ledger (hardware wallet like a flash drive. Has web-based front ends Ledger Live and Hive Ledger)

- Trezor (hardware wallet like a flash drive, similar to Ledger)

- Hive's front ends, Hive.io and PeakD, have their own wallets but also connect with Hive Ledger so that you can store your Hive on Ledger as well.

I started with web-based wallets and added a Ledger. Consider the same path because hacking and failures happen in crypto applications. Due to the projected increase in cybercrime and the high usage of these applications, especially as the bull run picks up, I recommend storing your crypto in several wallets. (Bitcoin and Ethereum emerge yet again as available on most wallets, and Hive emerges as having its wallets built into its major front ends and also available on Ledger.)

This is also why you must have your crypto exit plan together regarding wallets and exchanges before entering the crypto markets.

Chapter 6: Plan Your Exit FIRST

It has been said for many years: *"Failing to plan is planning to fail."* That reality goes into overdrive regarding crypto, and I have the crypto losses to prove it. But I'm not mad because my losses can become your gain! I can tell you from experience: plan your way out before you get into any position in crypto.

- Get your coins picked out: where you are getting them, what wallets they are going in, and how and when you are going to get them out before you buy them

- Some coins cannot be swapped back to USD directly, and that number may grow in the U.S.

- Some coins are unavailable on exchanges worldwide, meaning global accessibility does not exist equally for every coin. However, Bitcoin is tradable on crypto exchanges worldwide, and Ethereum is also widely available.

- Ensure you can get your coins back out through Bitcoin and Ethereum first, and through which exchanges you are going to do that.

Something else to remember as you set up for when you prepare to leave the market: there's what you want, what you need, and what is realistically possible based on the projects you choose and when you enter the market. Remember how we broke down the times in the cycle ahead?

- **Autumn 2023 to Spring 2024:** earliest time window to enter, although most of the crowd is still running away from the market in the last of the bear – biggest gains for the right projccts are possible from here.

- **Spring 2024 to Autumn 2024:** After the Bitcoin halving, members of the crowd that know about this begin to come back to the market, but the crowd as a mass is not ready yet – so the second-biggest gains are possible from here.

- **Autumn 2024 to Spring 2025:** The bull run begins in earnest, but still, the crowd is lagging a bit into the winter. There are still significant gains on some projects available, but the 100x gains you heard of before getting in here are gone because a year of preparation and positioning has gone by – you will buy what the early investors are selling from here.

- **Spring 2025 to Autumn 2025:** The wind up of the bull run – still good gains possible on good projects, but be careful. The top will likely form here, so do not intend to be greedy. Positioning yourself to get out is the most important thing.

- **Autumn 2025 and beyond:** get ready for the coming bull run of 2028 because you are most likely looking at the market from the top. There is no way to go but down through 2026 and most of 2027. (Kind of like what it is like in Summer 2023 when I am writing this, and like it was in Spring 2019 when I came in.)

But how do you leave, exactly? There are two steps, but the key is to develop the emotional discipline to follow them.

The first step is taking your investment out when you make a significant profit. Leave your *profit* exposed to changes in the market, not your *investment*. It will look different at different stages of the cycle.

For example, if you invest $100 well before Autumn 2024 in a good project, your investment has a good chance of doubling by Autumn 2024. In that case, take your first $100 out and leave the $100 profit through the rest of the run to your exit point. But if you invest later than Autumn 2024, you must be more modest depending on how long you have until Autumn 2025. This is when the bull run will likely end. If you invest $100 between Autumn 2024 and Spring 2025 in a good project, I suggest you make $150 your exit point for your investment.

In Spring 2025, some projects will likely begin to queue up to top out, a little before or after Bitcoin likely does in the mid-autumn of that year. If you invest $100 then, be content at $120 and even $110 if it is summertime, and take your investment out.

Remember: most people who will enter the crypto market in 2025 have yet to learn what the cycle is like. They will get off the fence because early investors will enjoy getting their initial investments back with some gains. Institutional investors will use the media to whip up interest to get the cycle where they want it for their exits. The crowd will bring their hopes and dreams and more money than they can afford to the market. Those who come in Winter 2024 will still be somewhat early and do well, but that will only feed the frenzy in the spring and summer that will lead to the top of the run in late 2025. By mid-2025, it will be time for prepared investors to make their final exit.

The final step is to take a percentage of your remaining profit out as you reach your investment goals until you exit your market position. You may be okay with doubling your profit, so when your $100 is $200, you can take it all and enjoy your life. You may think the market has a little bit more in it, or the project you are invested in has not peaked yet. In that case, take out a percentage of your profit and leave the rest for your hunch to be right or wrong.

The main thing is, do not leave your investment or the bulk of your profit in the market into 2026. A project, or two, or three, or five, may peak later than Bitcoin in Autumn 2025 – some peaks may form in early winter. Crypto is known for a few holiday presents at the tail end, but just a few. Much of Winter 2026 will see the crowd spending time in denial about the fact – unless the usual cycles break entirely – that the "only up" period of the previous two years is over. You do not want to be in that number because the stampede outward and the loss of 70-90 percent of the value in the market is coming.

The whole purpose for me, sitting and writing in Summer 2023, is to keep you out of the utter despair that the down half of the cycle in 2026 may well be. This is why the chapter on the exit plan comes before the chapter on the entrance plan. You must understand what to do and when to do it to avoid the mass exit that always comes at the end of the bull run. Leave on your own terms, not with the stampede!

Chapter 7: Now, Plan Your Entrance

The key to planning your entrance into the crypto markets is education. Here is what you need to do:

- Learn about where you can find the projects you want to get into.
- Learn about projects that have utility. Will they solve a problem or provide an opportunity?
- Learn about their usage. Have they been around for a cycle or more?
- Learn to see if a project has a good team that can execute what the project promises.

You can find all cryptos that have been around for a while on Coinmarketcap.com or Coingecko.com – I tend to look at both. You will find the average price across all exchanges. Those sites have news on there. Also, you will find what exchanges the coins are on, what wallets they use, and links to their project websites.

Next, go to the project websites. Usually, there is an "about" section, and there you will find whitepapers that tell you the design and goals of the project. Sometimes "**litepapers**" (summaries for everyday people if the project is tech-heavy) will be provided. You will also occasionally find a roadmap for the project through the next year of its development. You should also be able to find information on its founders and team. Run a Google search on the founders and team members, and check them out on LinkedIn and other social media if available.

It is essential to say here: if your gut tells you something is off about the founders or teams, even if you cannot say why you believe that, invest in something else. No matter how good the project looks, switch your investments. For example, in 2020, I sold an excellent project early because a team leader made some statements well outside of his expertise in crypto – comments I knew would encourage people to get themselves killed.

Crypto gathers interesting people who do interesting things under pressure, and 2020 was when most of us were under pressure. I accounted for that, of course. However, my gut was right in the summer of 2020. One in every one thousand people near the location of the activity he recommended during the pandemic was dead by December 2020. The stats hit the national news in the U.S.

I slept better in the winter of 2021, knowing my money was out of that project. I slept even better because I started buying the coin at around seven cents and left the market when the coin was around one dollar. The coin would reach around $2.50, but there are more gains between seven cents and a dollar than between $1 and $2.50. With a clear conscience, I sold to those who would get that 2.5x gain while I slept well on my 7x gain. The advantage of starting early and doing deep research is that your profit and conscience can be clear from the start to the finish.

Coinmarketcal.com is really Coin Market Calendar: you can search for cryptos by name and see what project news there is for them. You can commonly see updates and launches of dapps and Layer 2 projects and listings on exchanges and crypto events. You want to see if the project has some age and if there have been consistent progress updates through the bear. You also will want to see what updates are soon to come because prices generally go higher on the run-up to an update or event and fall afterward. You typically want to buy a little after an update to catch the rise, not the fall. Conversely, you should exit just before or during the last major Summer 2025 event. Why? The bull run will be nearly done by then, and the drop may keep dropping in that coin.

Solid articles from reputable investment sources for crypto can also be a good source of information. Coin Market Cap and Coin Gecko have articles, and here are some additional sources:

- Blockworks
- Altcoin Daily (also has a YouTube channel)
- AMBCrypto
- Admiral Markets (excellent educational content in “read more about cryptocurrency”)

There are a few solid crypto YouTubers as well. My rule is to look for channels that have consistently produced throughout the bear or, if they started in the spring or summer of 2023, are consistent. With all these, a caveat: *don’t follow crypto hype men.* Follow channels that talk about what the project is, what the project does, and can break down both why a coin is a good or bad choice to invest in from a charting perspective (price action) and fundamental perspective (what the project process is, what the news is, and where it is in the market cycle). Here are some thoughtful non-hype channels I listen to:

- Ben Cowen (YouTube)
- No BS Crypto (YouTube)
- Crypto Capital Venture (YouTube)
- Crypto Jebb (also has CT2A, YouTube)
- DataDash (YouTube)

Then, there is the Seizing the Crypto Bull Run newsletter that pulls all these resources together. You'll learn how to get that and save time on learning and choosing in Chapter 9.

Don't forget your exit plan in all this!

- We cannot predict the goings-on between now and Autumn 2025. Generally, all markets may recover if something big and bad happens in early 2024. Crypto shows that possibility in how the bull run recovered from the Spring 2020 impact of COVID-19. But we cannot say for sure when anything might happen.

- We cannot predict the impact of the U.S. general election in November 2024, which we know is going to happen.

- We cannot predict the exact nature of incoming regulations on the crypto market as a whole and on specific projects.

- We cannot predict particular projects being delisted (taken off a particular exchange) because of lousy action by the project team or incoming regulations.

- If you remember **NOTHING ELSE**, take your investment out when you have a significant profit!

You may have begun to realize by now that getting into the crypto market requires a bit of a lifestyle change, which is correct. Even before successful investors get the profits that change their lifestyles, they have changed how they spend their time and energy to get into, on top of, and, finally, out of their chosen investments. Things happen quickly in crypto, so doing well in the crypto market does require dedication.

However, by reading this book, you can take advantage of building on my dedication to understanding the markets in three ways:

1. Take all that you have read in this book and work to understand it well.

2. Pay close attention to the next chapter, Chapter 8; I will be sharing my personal strategy.

3. Pay close attention to Chapter 9; I will share how you can access an ongoing resource I am preparing for you in Summer 2023, along with this book.

Chapter 8: My Personal Strategy

Here are a couple of things to say: my personal strategy is, of course, my personal strategy. That is, it aligns with my personal goals and what I want to achieve in the crypto markets. I'm a quiet and peaceful person looking to live a quiet and peaceful life. I'm not in the crypto markets to get a Lamborghini.

I'm also not a financial advisor. I'm an artist, educator, and a journalist by profession. This is why, although I hold some Bitcoin, Ethereum, and Hive, I have not mentioned any of my other picks for the next bull run. A word of advice: Don't take investment advice from people who are not financial advisors. Don't even copy successful investors' moves without doing your own research, study, and preparation.

Remember: only you are you, and no one is living your life but you. Only you know what you can afford to invest and when. Only you can determine your goals and what and when you must invest. Crypto is about freedom, but freedom isn't free – it requires the courage to take command of your own life and move forward for yourself. You have plenty of time to sit down with yourself and determine what you need, what you want, and what is realistic for you to invest.

Part of my personal strategy is to get to my favorite places in the world and be quiet there. I think, pray, and write down my ideas, plans, and goals. I noted the idea for this book in my journal, in the last days of July 2023, and then I wrote the outline of this book by hand in that same journal in August. Once I had the idea, I determined what I wanted, what I needed, and what was realistic, and then set to work day after day. I suggest the same approach before entering the crypto market.

I am, by temperament, a deliberative person. I love what Abraham Lincoln said about chopping down trees: "If you have six hours to chop down a tree, spend four hours sharpening the axe." Because of this, I am a long-term swing trader on most things and an investor on a few coins. (And again, you can probably guess what those coins are.) I prefer to take early positions and let the market cycle do the work in giving me my profits.

Considering what Bitcoin, Ethereum, and Hive offer gives you a good idea of the kinds of coins I look at. I focus on coins with a track record that already shows that they have utility and usage. I'm interested in decentralization because I'm interested in freedom. I'm interested in fair, transparent access to crypto's value and in doing business without being beholden to the legacy corporate and financial system. I recognize that Bitcoin and Ethereum's fees are high, and the systems are sometimes slow.

So, I look at a fair number of projects that improve access for a price that works worldwide while not throwing quality to the winds. Hive stands out in that respect.

I look at projects that prove themselves to be able to work well with existing systems like the supply chain and the business community. I also look at projects that help different blockchains communicate and work together.

Then, I look at crypto charts to see what they have done in the last cycle and what they are likely to do in this one, also looking at their news in between. Does their team believe in what they are doing enough to have kept doing it? In other words, does the chain still have developers making progress in what can be done on the chain? Was there a scandal in this bear around the project or any previous ones? How are and how have the team leaders been behaving through the bear? Have they shown good leadership of the project?

One of the things I also consider as a long-term swing trader is the control of taxes. Although I am not a tax advisor, I know that in the United States in 2023, if you hold a capital gain for a year and one day, you don't have to pay capital gains taxes on the first $40,525. So, I will owe only regular income taxes if I get out of a position I've held for a year and a day before I have $40,525 in profit – *this means I avoid double taxation on the same money.*

I learned from Robert Kiyosaki a long time ago that controlling taxes is a key to financial freedom because the fewer taxes you owe, the more profit you keep. Nothing is stopping me from selling every crypto I don't intend to stay in for $40,524 in profit and not paying capital gains taxes on any one of them, provided I have held each of those cryptos a year and a day. That is another reason I start early – really early!

I do not invest in what are called "**meme coins.**" Dogecoin is the oldest of these. In the last cycle, it had many copies, copies of copies, and copies of copies of copies. The Binance Smart Chain was full of them. Their communities tend to be full of people who are moved by charismatic figures who make it their business to manipulate the price. Usually, those prices cannot live past the hype. Then there are projects in which the founders go into the main wallet, take everything that has been invested, and bankrupt the coin. These are called "**rug pulls**" because the founders of these scams pull the rug right out from under all those who believe and invest in the projects.

Don't get me wrong. There is money to be made in meme coins, money of the type that is made by taking candy from babies. I sat and watched the cycle start in Dogecoin as people announced that they would make it do a certain thing to show the power of the community. Later, they waited for their favorite personality to say something that moved the price. I watched more experienced traders position themselves, wait until the announced date, and sell to those running in before the crash. I watched these things play out on crypto charts again and again—a predictable and sad exploitation of human nature by those who know how markets work. If I were a short-term trader and had the seared conscience necessary to take candy from babies, I'd be all over meme coins.

I do owe the existence of meme coins this: the market behavior around them is a fast-forward display of how the whole crypto cycle tends to work. More experienced traders get positioned before the crowd comes in. From where I sit writing in Summer 2023, almost any decently positioned coin will have gains from the last of the bear. I am writing this book now because meme coins gave me a mental model of how people do badly when they are late to the cycle. The difference is the crypto market as a whole has value in it. Bitcoin, Ethereum, and Hive have proven themselves to improve people's lives by virtue of what they are and what they do, not due to their price at a particular time. I cannot name a single meme coin that, past the hype train, is more than a money pit.

I also tend to avoid the crowd generally; it is too late when the public has found its way in mass into a market. By the time Bitcoin and Ethereum are in the mainstream news, it is too late for those who watch the news to see the largest gains because experienced investors are 1-2 years ahead of them and have caught the entire run-up. Again, this is why I am writing this book in Summer 2023: I want you to have the chance to get as close to having the advantages I have as possible. You and I do not have to compete for this large opportunity to move toward financial freedom. There is enough for everyone.

There's one more resource I would like to recommend to you. If you have read this far, I thank you for trusting me. And if you have trusted me thus far, you'll want to read on to see what else I am doing to level the playing field.

Chapter 9: The SCBRFF Newsletter

If you have read this far, I thank you. You have found value in the information about the coming crypto bull cycle and my approach to sharing it with you. If you see value in continuing to hear from me, I invite you to subscribe to the Seizing the Crypto Bull Run for Financial Freedom Newsletter, known from here on out as the SCBRFF Newsletter.

What the SCBRFF Newsletter Will Do for You

The SCBRFF Newsletter will feature information to deepen your understanding of Bitcoin, Ethereum, and Hive. It will also discuss projects that fit this book's utility, usage, and strong team rubric.

The SCBRFF Newsletter will feature news and analysis from around the crypto world from the respected publications and solid YouTube channels mentioned in this book. This will be complete with my breakdown and commentary focused on getting you the necessary information to make clear decisions for yourself.

The SCBRFF Newsletter will keep you abreast of conferences and events in and around the crypto world so you can gather your information and meet the communities around different projects LIVE if you so choose.

The SCBRFF Newsletter will present a roundup of coins and projects mentioned in each edition, where you can get them, what wallets you can put them in, and where you can get deeper information about them.

The first edition of the SCBRFF Newsletter comes out on the day of the publication of this book, October 30, 2023. It will appear biweekly until the Bitcoin halving, now estimated to occur by or around April 16, 2024. Because of the increase of crypto news at that time and following through the rest of the new cycle, the SCBRFF Newsletter will most likely change to a weekly schedule after the Bitcoin halving, late in the spring of 2024. All previous editions to whenever you subscribe will be archived and available to you.

But WHY?

You're smart. If you have read this book, you are also wise and thoughtful in approaching financial freedom for yourself, and you want to make moves in crypto that fit your goals. You can take this book and do everything you need to do, just like I did in discovering all the things that have gone into this book.

I remember the time it required to gain the mastery I am sharing with you and the mistakes I made for needing to learn more soon enough. The SCBRFF Newsletter is designed to save you time getting in before the crowd, getting into the projects you want, and getting out before the crash.

Your investment into continuing education in what is going on in the crypto markets and around the crypto world is a wise investment in yourself and your future success. The $20 a month you decide to invest in yourself, and your future success in subscribing to the SCBRFF Newsletter can be the gateway to help you find crypto projects that will richly reward your investment and find them on time.

Now, you're smart. You can save the $20 a month and figure things out independently like I did. I also think you are smart enough, if you have read this far, to know that time is of the essence and that if you have found value in this book, the SCBRFF Newsletter will be an extension of the value.

Your First Crypto-Related Call to Action!

For everyone who reads this book, the SCBRFF Newsletter will only be $20 a month. That's the introductory price for the autumn of 2023 worldwide, and for all my readers, that's the price. People discovering the newsletter after Spring 2024 may have to pay significantly more! So, again, I'm offering you a massive head start on the crowd in every way! It's now decision time for you!

Go right ahead and sign up for the SCBRFF Newsletter at https://scrbff-newsletter.beehiiv.com/upgrade. My team on Beehiiv will collect the appropriate information and get you immediate access to all the issues available at the introductory price of $20 a month (or $200 per year, a savings on two months!) Get that done, and enjoy your SCBRFF Path 1 status. You seized the opportunity to get this book and continue your learning, and you are on your way now to seize the crypto bull run!

One More Added-Value Thing…

Suppose you want to seize the crypto bull run in a way that is organic to you as a creative person... Remember me telling you about Hive, the Proof-of-Brain blockchain? The epilogue is your guide to learning and earning crypto in the most democratic, decentralized way possible through blogging/social media. How to get your account, what to do with your first crypto keys, how to get a faster start than average, what to post first, and more is up ahead!

Epilogue: Seizing the Best Possible Start on Hive

You Are in the Matrix, For Real ...

Did you know that by using everyday social media – often referred to as Web 2 – you are building a business and a bank?

It's just not *your* business or *your* bank...

If you promote your business, you will pay ad costs that eat into your revenue without guaranteeing a return. But your everyday use provides an excellent outlet for social media to run ads that pay the corporations in charge.

These corporations use social media to keep information about you that you provide. They can remix any content you share without your permission to promote their business. (That's in the fine print of most terms of use.) Also, they can sell the data you give them to their partners for big money. They also use your data to advertise to you. Some put what is called a "cookie" on your choice of hardware to track other buying decisions you are making.

These corporations also work hand in hand with law enforcement and other government agencies to track what users do and say. While this is not always bad, consider what happens if your government turns away from the principles of democracy and free speech and decides that you are an enemy of the state.

Those are the stakes you work with daily on social media. You are building other people's businesses, bank accounts, and surveillance apparatuses with your thoughts, creativity, and content. Now, these platforms offer you large audiences and reach, but understand the other side of the coin.

But what if I told you there was a community-run decentralized way to do all major forms of blogging, microblogging, and video creation? What if I told you that you could be handed the keys to the business and bank portions, where nobody is selling your data and privacy to the highest bidder?

I've already told you about it. That's the Hive blockchain, considered from the viewpoint of its social front ends.

Ready To Own a Business and a Bank of Your Own?

Hive's major social front ends are PeakD, Hive.io, and Ecency for mixed media long-form posting. Liketu is a front-end for photography (although a ton of this is just done on the long-form front ends, too). Leothreads and Ecency Waves are front-ends for microblogging. Threespeak, Cast Garden, and Dbuzz are front-ends for video posting. Cast Garden is also set up for podcasting and syndication to the decentralized Fediverse (the veterans of decentralized content).

There are other ways onto Hive as well; there are games, art platforms, and more. However, the long-form blogging front ends offer the most flexibility, and once you have your cryptographic keys set up, you can use them to get into anything else.

Yes, I said **cryptographic keys** – the keys to the business and bank you are getting into when you start on Hive. You choose what you post, and you keep ownership of it. You decide what to do with what the community chooses to mine for you of Hive. You can spend it, save it, invest it for yourself, or lend it out to other projects – or do all of that simultaneously. Hive can be thought of as offering every user the personal option of owning a business and a bank. As you should expect, there is a bit more security than on your everyday social media, where it is easy for you to walk in and leave your stuff in someone else's custody.

There's also a bit more to think about: businesses take a good deal of consistent work and a fair amount of time invested to take off. From a banker's perspective, banking takes thinking about making money work hard beyond immediate consumption. People miss out on all the benefits of Hive because they do not understand a real-life principle: businesses and banks have to be built up before they can yield solid returns. Hive is an excellent small-scale practice for what every entrepreneur and investor must learn to do well over the long run.

The Proof-of-Brain concept for blockchain works out to obtain crypto-like sweat equity in a business. If you come only bringing your talents and interests, and content creation skills, you will have to work on Hive to turn those into a foundation for big profit at the end of the bull run or sustainable passive income through all seasons. There are easier ways to get crypto. But to me, none has been more personally rewarding from the end of the last bear to now. In this epilogue, I'll share the foundational steps and the mindset necessary to master them.

Of the long-form front-ends on Hive that I have used, I prefer PeakD because of its powerful features on both the creation and the business/bank sides of the work. You'll find PeakD's entrance portal at https://peakd.com, and when you get there, you will see the logo and two buttons: "How It Works" and "Join Now." Read the whole page to the bottom first, and then come back and push the "How It Works" button first and watch the video.

Ensure you have the best understanding possible, and don't push the "Join Now" button until you decide…

Desktop/Laptop or Mobile?

A lot goes wrong with joining Hive through any front end because of not planning like one will own a little business and bank. This means you must decide what you will be doing on Hive and whether it works best for you on a desktop or mobile computer. This will also come up again when you get your crypto keys and make transactions in your wallet.

I prefer a desktop because I enjoy writing on Hive and have made that the engine of my business and bank – I do some photography, music, and visual art. Still, my business is writing, and that holds everything together. Regarding access and security for the bank portion, copying and pasting keys into login portals is harder on the phone, as is making other copies and putting them in backup places not connected to the Internet at all times. I also have a dedicated laptop that I don't take out except for other business – so I don't keep my keys on my laptop. I make sure to log out when I make a rare excursion with it, and I don't keep my keys on my phone I take out all the time. So, the chances of those keys getting into the wrong hands are small.

Again, my thinking is based on looking at the end from the beginning. From Summer 2023, still in the bear market, it is not possible for anyone not familiar with the market to understand how much cybercrime will be occurring by 2025, as people who don't care to do things the right way will still want their share of the profits at our expense. Because of the nature of my business and my thoughts on security, I choose to access Hive through a laptop. Your business may differ, so how you set up the banking part may be another. It is for you to decide, but it is a serious decision to make.

Joining and Getting Your Keys

Once you decide whether to primarily access Hive on a computer or mobile device, you can hit "Join Now" and make your first business decision. If you are into gaming and like role-playing game setups, Splinterlands will set you up with your account and the basic things you need to start. PeakD refers to it on the $10 link. The other two options I'll discuss here stay in PeakD. Hivedex will set up an anonymous account for you at $1, and Hive Onboard will do so for free. This is your first major decision.

How do you want your business and bank set up? Blockchains are very open affairs. A regular Hive account will allow people to ask and find the answer to "What's in your wallet?" Again, that means little in the bear market. But if you are one of those who get off to a good start and tend to thrive while others struggle, you could be a standout by bull run time! Do you want to stand out, or would you prefer to let your business be hidden from public view? That's the difference between Hive Onboard and Hivedex.io. A difference of $1 today gives you two completely different paths to what people know about you in the future. This is not a choice I had in 2020, but you have it now, *although for an absolute beginner, it is still easier to use Hive Onboard, because you need that $1 in crypto to pay HiveDex.io.* You will need to have at least $20 in Bitcoin in a wallet somewhere to pay HiveDex.io $1 … but remember the chapters I already wrote on how to get onto an exchange, buy crypto, and get it into a wallet?

When you decide between HiveDex.io and Hive Onboard, the next screen you see will have instructions. Read them all, and then you will have an opportunity to pick your username. This is your next business decision: what will your (brand) identity be on Hive? I stand by my written work with my name on Hive as I do on this book – my name is my brand if you will. People pick their online names for many reasons, but remember: if you want to change it on Hive, you must start a new account! So, choose wisely.

After you pick your username, read all instructions, and then you will see your screen of keys. When I explained Bitcoin, I explained that the whole Proof-of-Work concept operates by decoding cryptographic hashes, which are long strings of alphanumeric characters. These strings of letters and numbers show up everywhere in cryptocurrency. Your wallet and exchange addresses for different coins will have you copying these long strands back and forth so your funds can get to where they need to go. Hive, being both a business and a bank, has four strands as keys for different functions on the chain.

- **Master (or Owner) Key:** This long strand is the parent of the remaining three rearrangements with different power levels. The Master Key can authorize all possible functions available on the Hive blockchain. Treat this like your spare house key. Don't put this one into any application on Hive; this level of authorization is only needed for changing all keys.

- **Active Key:** This key involves all transactions involving moving your funds on the chain. Because PeakD has your Hive Wallet attached, you only need to share this key with any application outside of PeakD and your choice of login/transaction app once you are ready to branch way out on the blockchain. This is your bank vault combination. Treat it as such.

- **Posting Key:** This is the key that allows you to do all interactions with Hive's front ends from day to day. This gives authorization to PeakD and other front ends to post your content. This one is designed to be used in other apps, but still, BE CAREFUL. Between the two login/transaction apps I will discuss later in the chapter, you already have enough with your posting key to log into all front ends on Hive.

- **Memo Key:** This is rarely used, but should someone send you an encoded memo along with a transaction on Hive in your wallet, pull this out to decode it.

These four keys are the keys to your Hive business and bank, and this is where a laptop or desktop shines: when you see the key screen, IMMEDIATELY screenshot it or copy and paste it into a text document. Please save it to an external drive or two or three but not to your phone or computer connected to the Internet, and print a paper copy to keep in a safe place. Have plenty of backup copies on this because there is no "forgot password?" option on Hive. If you lose your keys and any associated passwords you choose to make up for other apps, no one on a decentralized blockchain has the authority or access to help you. You will be permanently locked out of your account. Don't let it happen to you. Make plenty of backup copies of your four keys, and store them safely offline.

Then, you will be prompted to choose how you want to log in to PeakD. If you are on a laptop/desktop, I recommend HiveSigner or Hive Keychain (which can be downloaded to a Firefox, Chrome, or Brave browser). If you are on mobile, I recommend Hive Keychain Mobile. You will need to copy at least your posting key in here, and when you get ready to make money moves, you also need to put your active key in one of these.

Once you have chosen and set up your login app, you will be taken into your fresh, new PeakD account!

I've done a walkthrough for you on YouTube – it's UNLISTED to the rest of the world, but YOU, as a book reader, can access it at the end of this chapter!

SCBRFF Tip 1: Free is Good, but Fast is BETTER

Only some on Hive have dared to share this because, REMEMBER: Hive is free to join. It is free to use, but what is rarely explained is that you need "resource credits" to transact on the chain. To make your first post, you will need enough resource credits, or RC, to move around on the chain.

You can only get resource credits by having Hive staked on the chain. You need at least 15 Hive staked up as Hive Power to do a daily post and thank five people who greet you daily.

If you use the link I will provide you for Hive Onboard, PeakD will let me know (eventually). Then, I'll do my banker thing and delegate the 15 Hive Power to you (that's a bank loan in Hive terms) when I find out if I can. I expect this book to be successful, so it could come to a point in 2024 that I can't delegate enough for everyone – so, first come, first serve. Here is my referral link, right here:

https://peakd.com/register?ref=scrbffreaders1

But imagine coming onto Hive and having no one to help you – or waiting days or weeks. This is why onboarding to Hive is a challenge: it is not easy for people to get started because if you don't have resource credits, how will you build?

I'm going to cut the knot that cannot be untied. I recommend PeakD to you because, on the first day, you can go into your wallet, buy the 15 Hive, power them up, and get onto the rest of what you need to do. At this moment, at the end of the bear market in crypto, 15 Hive are worth around $4.15. Pretend Hive is $2, and the cost is $30.

When you get into your PeakD account, go to the menu under your username and click "Wallet" in it. Scroll down until you see the button marked "Buy Hive." Click "Use CC," and you will be taken to the Transak page that works with PeakD. At this moment, Hive is around 30 cents, so 15 Hive will run you about $4.50, but the lowest dollar amount you can put into Transak is $30. That, today, will get you around 103 Hive. Until Hive reaches $2, this method will always get you more Hive than you need to get started.

But REMEMBER: think like a business owner and banker.

You can power all of that Hive up, and that will make a difference when you vote on other people's posts. You will then have enough to earn tiny curation rewards on every post you vote on. Half of all post rewards are paid out to curators, the people who read and vote.

Powering all that Hive up will allow you to write as many posts and comments daily and weekly as needed. 50 Hive, for most people, is enough: that gives you enough resources and credits to do about three posts and sixteen comments a day.

If you choose to power up less Hive than you buy, you can also go into SimpleSwap (under "Others Services" the PeakD) and swap the remainder for your first Bitcoin or Ethereum (if you have your wallets for those set up).

Yes, you read that right. Hive can be exchanged for Bitcoin and Ethereum in the PeakD wallet through partners Transak and Simpleswap without reference to a big centralized exchange. I told you that Hive is a business and a bank, and PeakD is the most powerful front end for it. This means you have three options to maximize your whole $30. You also now know-how, as the end of the next run approaches (because remember, we plan the exit before the entrance), how to trade any Hive you wish to take profit on into Bitcoin and Ethereum and then take those onto an exchange that will allow you to sell for your local currency.

After purchasing your Hive, wait a few minutes and refresh your wallet. You should see the Hive at the top of your account. Click on the menu by the number, and select "Power Up." A screen will open to allow you to choose how much you want to power up. I recommend powering up 15-50 Hive to start, but it is entirely your decision. Once you have done that, you are ready to make moves on Hive.

Again, this way of starting on Hive is controversial because Hive is free. When people come in, they are invited by people and communities that give them the boost they need to get started on a free basis, and it is lovely. I believe in that, but I also think this book will reach more people than I can personally help, so help yourself to Hive with this first quick-start method.

SCBRFF Tip No. 2: Be a Good Neighbor

So, let's recap: say you went to PeakD and chose the type of account you wanted from either Hivedex.io or HiveOnboard, and then got your username, got your keys, secured them, and then chose how you would get Hive Power and, thus, resource credits into your account.

Surprisingly, the next step is *not* to write your first post. The next step is to become familiar with Hive's communities and determine where you will most be at home to recoup your $30 investment and build from there. Go to https://peakd.com/communities and enjoy what you can choose from. There's something for every passion and interest.

I recommend that you join the Hive Learners Community and the OCD Community at the beginning: these communities have resources that will help you learn how best to move successfully. They are also the right place to put your introductory post, but we will get to that later. Each community has a "Subscribe" button: hit that, and you're in!

As for other communities, you can come in and hang out just like you do on social media. But since this is a book about seizing the crypto bull run, you will need to assess these communities in a way that honors your interests and also your investment. There are three steps to this:

Click on any and every community that meets your interest. The more, the better.

As you check out the communities, consider what subjects you are passionate enough to produce content about regularly: once a week, a few times a week, or daily. It's up to you, but understand that Hive does not reward inconsistency.

Consider each community for the number of subscribers compared with consistent active users and rewards, often at $1.00 or more across a number of users. $1 is a baseline, attainable even in the bear – but should you read this in Spring 2024 or later, make that baseline $3-10. That level of consistent rewards means the community has strong curation support, so if you consistently do quality work, you consistently have the opportunity to learn and earn.

Once you have 3-4 communities that fit the above criteria in addition to joining Hive Learners and OCD, spend some time reading in all of these communities. Take a week and engage with the content creators you like. Follow all the ones you want. Ask questions if you are learning, and give thoughtful compliments about what you liked in posts you enjoyed. If you have powered up 50 Hive or more, you can comment about 30 times daily and vote on each post you want. This is a great way to make new friends and practice the consistent work you will need to do when you decide to start posting and responding to comments on your posts. This is also how you will begin building an organic following.

If you do nothing else on Hive but vote and comment on other people's posts, eventually, your curation rewards will recoup your $30 investment because your vote will pay out, and people may choose to vote and reward your good comments.

After a week, when you can gauge the engagement around your engagement, join the communities you are most comfortable with. Keep engaging until you can make your introductory post, best done in Hive Learners or GEMS Community. Every community has a "Create a Post" button, but before you hit that, there are a few more things you need to do first.

SCBRFF Tip 3: The Big Four and Your Intro Post

On Hive, everyone is encouraged to make an introductory post. If you do it right and in the right community, help and rewards will find you. Four things to consider right from the start:

- Hive has a zero-tolerance stance on plagiarism. You do not want to test this on Hive. Make sure that what you write is what you wrote and that you use your photos or artwork from sites that allow such use and cite them properly. Four are below:

    - Unsplash

- Pixabay
- Pexels
- Wikimedia Commons

- Hive has many communities that have a zero-tolerance policy on AI-generated content. If, by chance, you are an artist who works AI into your digital art, the Alien Art Hive Community can be a home. But even then, you will need to be able to show your steps and originality added to it. It is best to avoid AI-generated content on Hive as a new Hiver.

- Although there is no posted requirement about this, my experience on Hive suggests that the minimum requirement for a post to be considered quality is 200 original words and/or three photos with commentary about them, summing to at least 100 words. Are you doing a video on YouTube and going to talk about it on PeakD? Add 100-200 original words with that.

- Do not spam. Also, be careful reusing content you have published elsewhere. Hive prioritizes original, first-use content. Whatever you bring, add at least 100-200 new words centered on the community you are writing in.

All businesses and banks have regulations they must follow to operate. Although Hive does not have a technical book of rules, Hive's membership chooses what it will and will not reward, and these are the BIG FOUR issues besides onboarding itself. If you ignore these, no one will take your content down, and you can still share it on other platforms. Still, you will be locked out of the reward pool and eventually not be visible anywhere but on your blog page because communities and individuals will mute you from being seen on their page feeds.

What you want to do on Hive is avoid hustling backward. If you mess with the Big Four, it will take you a year or more to recover, and you will not enjoy the work with Hivewatchers and community leaders. That's the best I've seen on recovery time when recoveries happen. Think like a business person or a banker: when you break the rules, you pay the price in a lost opportunity to earn and grow. Hive is no different. Do not test Hive's community on the Big Four.

Let's talk about what to do in all the incredible space you have left to do a magnificent, eye-catching intro post! You already know you will need at least 200 words and three photos… but this is about YOU and the story of YOU. What's your story? What do you want Hive to know about you? What identity (or brand identity) do you have that you may want to emphasize? What are your three best selfies, three best pictures of your family and friends, and three best pictures of you doing what you love enough for the world to know about it? (you don't need nine images, but pick at least three.) What are your hobbies and interests that you love sharing about? Do you have a video of you doing your thing? Do you have a resource you have built that you can mention that Hive members may be interested in knowing about?

What's your story? Pull it together. Space out those selfies, family, friends, and you-doing-you photos, artworks, and videos with 200 words about your story. You will never get a second chance to make a first impression! Go big! Add a bold headline at the top!

Here is the technical part to let you get your post seen: in PeakD, there is a tag box under where you will put the body of your first post. You can include ten tags. In this tag box, ensure you have the tags introduceyourself, introduction, and intro-post, and then fill out tags related to your interest areas. Pro tip: go back, look into the communities you've joined, and find common use tags to add to your ten tags.

Don't hit publish yet – take a break, walk away, and come back and edit your post. PeakD has a spell-checker that will highlight common mistakes. Make sure you catch all those and also make sure you have stated all the sources of where you got your photos and artwork. Make sure your story for Hive is all that you want it to be – and then hit Publish! You will have just completed your first post on Hive!

SCBRFF Tip 4: The Square Deal Plan

I have been on Hive and its predecessor for four years. That's four years through two bears, so I have a good idea now about how to learn, earn, and build community simultaneously in all states of the market. Four is also the number of sides on a square, so I call this the Square Deal Plan. Take the first part as an ideal – you can only do half or a quarter of this plan right now. Someday, you may be able to do much more. But the point here is a four-step plan to get content consistently done, and your presence known and voted up in a way that supports the communities you join and Hive as a whole.

- Join up to four communities with a high ratio of active users to subscribers, where a good number of posts meet the baseline of at least $1 in rewards (in addition to Hive Learners and GEMS).

- Read at least four posts a week in each of the communities you are in (16 posts per week in total, or a bit more than two per day) to understand what community members are passionate about.

- Comment meaningfully and vote up all the posts you like, but do not let that number fall below four posts a week across all communities, meaning that you will give no less than 16 votes and meaningful comments per month on Hive.

- Post in each community once a week (four posts a week in total, 16 posts per month).

Even if you scale this down by four – say you found one community, and you only have time to do one post right now – the key to this plan is your adding value to the community all the time by consistently curating (reading, thoughtfully commenting, and voting) and making your presence known on Hive as an active member who adds value to each community you join.

Many people come to Hive in need, posting up in need of the rewards Hive's community can provide through voting up their posts. Then they take the rewards and apply those rewards to living their lives. I understand that. It has been a difficult three years for the whole world, and there is no end to the difficulty in sight for many.

However, no community, anywhere, wants to be used, and Hive is no exception. I know how much resentment there is toward people who just come to take and do not engage meaningfully with the rest of the community. The Square Deal Plan, therefore, is how you never come up in that discussion and have an easier path to being at home on Hive.

Speaking of a square deal, Hive offers you that too. The reason I recommend that you survey communities for a baseline of rewards and engagement is because when you see those reward numbers, you need to divide by four:

- One-fourth of the rewards is paid to the author in HBD, meaning the author can stake them up for 20 percent interest.

- One-fourth of the rewards are paid to the author in Hive Power. This means the author gets more stake to make more and bigger votes. They get to make more posts and comments, leave some on the account to make about three percent interest, or delegate out to other curation projects for passive Hive or Layer 2 project income (remember, on Hive, you own a BANK).

- Two-fourths – or one-half – of the rewards are spread between everyone who voted on the post in Hive Power (which is how you get rewards for just voting, too). This means that all those people get more HP, so they can make more and bigger votes, make more posts and comments, and delegate more to other projects.

Hive has its own "rule of four," and I have structured how we talk about it in this epilogue to prepare you mentally for that reality. There is no get-rich-quick plan for Hive, but there is a Square Deal Plan for you based on Hive's rule of four.

Now, about getting up to four posts a week: if you noticed, PeakD has a big green "Schedule" button when you publish your introduction post near the big blue "Publish" button. In other words, if you want to, you can prepare all your posts for one community on one or two days of the month and then schedule them out over the coming weeks if you like. This gives you the luxury of setting up a consistent post schedule without creating each day to meet that schedule. You can, therefore, take a few days a month and set up all your posts in a particular community.

PeakD also has a draft box, so if you don't finish what you are doing in one day, you can leave it in Drafts. You'll find your drafts and scheduled posts in the menu that has the little pencil. That one will let you create a post for your blog, view your drafts or your scheduled posts, and, when you are ready to do more advanced regular posts, even set up templates for those!

The SCBRFF Exclusive Playlist on YouTube

Would you like a walkthrough of how to set up your account and get it funded? How about a walkthrough on how to find communities and set up your introductory post? Here they are!

How to Get the Best Start on PeakD: https://youtu.be/xQ5ao_x5uD0

Communities and Introductory Post Setup: https://youtu.be/hMHerGIxI0g

Also, check out the entire SCBRFF playlist – unlisted to the world but available to you, and to be added to as you drop comments on things you'd like to see!

https://www.youtube.com/playlist?list=PLAZ7z7GcAQPL9tVqMGA49-wi24pzA8IvD

That's all, folks – that's it on Hive and except for the glossary of terms, that's it for this entire book! Thank you for reading *Seizing the Crypto Bull*

Run for Financial Freedom. Now, go seize this coming (or present, if you are reading in Spring 2024 or later) crypto bull run – best to you!

Glossary of Terms

Altcoins: all crypto coins that are not Bitcoin, short for "alternative coins"

Bear market: popular term borrowed from the stock market to describe a market that has crashed at least 20 percent and stays down consistently. In crypto, this type of market can persist for as much as two years, with a 70-90 percent crash being common!

Bitcoin: the first cryptocurrency and blockchain system, with each unit of Bitcoin created through decoding its unique cryptographic hash. Its symbol on exchanges for its cryptocurrency is **BTC.**

Blockchain: like a digital ledger, a list of all cryptocurrency transactions, with one transaction (or "block") being recorded and validated after another in a chain of transactions, hence the name "blockchain."

Bull market: popular term borrowed from the stock market to describe a market that has risen at least 20 percent and continues to rise consistently. In crypto, this type of market can persist for as much as two years, but then is followed by an equally long and savage bear market!

Centralized exchanges: exchanges on which crypto is bought and sold that are controlled by a single power (usually, a for-profit corporation)

Crypto exchanges: places online to buy, sell, and swap cryptocurrencies

Crypto wallets (hot and cold): where you store your cryptocurrency, in a similar manner to an online bank account. Each wallet has its own address on the blockchain. A "hot" wallet is generally connected to the Internet, and a "cold" wallet works more like a flash drive: you plug it in, send your crypto to it, and then unplug it from your computer and store it securely.

Cryptographic hash: a piece of data, like a message or a file, turned into a fixed-length string of letters and numbers. This code, or hash, is unique for each piece of data.

Cryptographic keys: cryptographic hashes used as key phrases that computers use to keep information safe and private, information including access to and transactions on different blockchains and dapps.

Dapps: Short for decentralized applications, without corporation or other single authority point of ownership and user information storage.

Decentralized: Without a single authority or failure point, often run by distributed computing assets (lots of servers in lots of different locations)

Decentralized exchanges: exchanges for crypto that run by algorithm, with no corporation or other single authority point or ownership

Electronic mining: how new cryptocurrency coins are created through using computer power to solve complex math problems and verify transactions on the blockchain.

Ethereum: the second cryptocurrency and blockchain system, and the first altcoin because it is the first alternative coin to Bitcoin. Its symbol on exchanges for its cryptocurrency is **ETH.**

Fiat money: money printed by governments not using a gold or silver standard to back their currencies up, only valuable as long as people agree that it is. "Fiat" means "by will."

Forking: When members of a particular crypto project decide to move in a different direction using the same blockchain technology, they can turn one chain into two or more separate projects that came or "forked" from the original. For example, the Steem blockchain now has two forks, the most prominent of which is the Hive blockchain.

Gas fees: Term used for transaction fees on the Ethereum blockchain, fees necessary to do anything on the chain.

Halving event: An algorithmic pattern in Bitcoin that cuts the amount of Bitcoin available to be mined in half, every four years.

Hard money: Currencies that have a fixed number of units that will ever be created, and therefore are incapable of inflation. Bitcoin is considered the first cryptographically based hard money, with a fixed supply of 21 million Bitcoins.

Layer 1: a blockchain whose technology and cryptocurrency serves as a base for other applications and blockchains built on it. Those projects are often referred to as **Layer 2** projects.

Long-term traders: traders that buy and hold projects for months and years, often with the entire length of the crypto market cycle in mind.

Ledger: A record of cryptocurrency transactions, public and immutable (can't be erased). Also, Ledger is the name of a cold, offline crypto wallet.

Meme coins: Cryptocurrencies that begin based on internet memes, funny images, or certain famous personalities. Meme coins tend to have their moment of communities coming up around and hyping them but, they are not as stable an investment as Bitcoin or any serious cryptocurrency project.

Proof-of-Brain: A blockchain that issues new units of its cryptocurrency through community validation of content, activity, and dapp work created on the chain. Hive is the best-known cryptocurrency of this type.

Proof-of-Work: A blockchain that issues new units of its cryptocurrency through the work of solving and validating (called mining) of cryptographic units. Bitcoin is the first and best-known cryptocurrency of this type.

Proof-of-Stake: A blockchain that issues new units of its cryptocurrency and permits governance of the chain based on how much of the existing cryptocurrency users have staked (stored long-term) on the chain. Ethereum is now the best-known cryptocurrency of this type, though it began as Proof-of-Work.

Rug pull: When founders steal all of the investment in a particular project, therefore pulling the rug out from under investors.

Satoshis: Divisions of Bitcoin, named for Bitcoin's creator Satoshi Nakamoto. Similar to how each U.S. dollar has 100 cents, each Bitcoin contains 100 million Satoshis.

Short-term traders: Traders that buy and hold projects for days and weeks, looking for patterns and trends that lead to quick profit.

Soft money: Currencies with no limit to how many units of it can be printed, so inflation possibilities are infinite.

Stablecoins: Cryptocurrencies designed to have each unit be equivalent with a national fiat currency.

Staking: Long-term saving of a particular cryptocurrency on its own blockchain, often rewarded with interest and governance privileges.

Supply shock: An unexpected change in how much of something is available. In the context of Bitcoin, a supply shock occurs after halving events because the amount of new Bitcoin available for the future has been cut in half.

Whitepapers and litepapers: A whitepaper is a comprehensive explanation of a cryptocurrency, including how its blockchain works and what opportunity or problem the project is meant to address. A litepaper is a shorter, less technical summary of a project's whitepaper.

www.ingramcontent.com/pod-product-compliance
Lightning Source LLC
LaVergne TN
LVHW022008200926
848481LV00007B/2284
* 9 7 8 1 7 3 5 5 7 5 2 1 6 *